So I Just Got Saved. Now What?!

a VERY practical guide to being a Christian today

Donte Allen

Bennett Publishing Company

Published by: Bennett Publishing Company
Contact: www.Donteallen.com/contact/
https://www.facebook.com/DonteAllenTheWriter/

Visit the author's website at www.DonteAllen.com
Printed in the U.S.A.

First Edition: July 2018
ISBN:0692157735
Reviewed by: John Kempf
Reviewed and Edited by: Tracy Mann

10   9   8   7   6   5   4   3   2   1

To My Brother and Sisters,

Keep the faith and stay humble yo.

May this book find you well in your walk with God, and may it encourage you to press on.

This book is dedicated to my wife, Teshona. Your love has spurred me on to reach the potential that God has given me. Your encouragement and support help me to keep Jesus as my center, and to love those around me. Thank you.

-your love story

Contents

Introduction

YO!!! Praise the Lord Family!!! I want to welcome you to the family of God! It's truly amazing to know that the family of heaven is growing rapidly, and that you are now a part of this family. I want you to know that you've made an incredible life changing decision, and things in your life are going to change in an amazing way. Now that Jesus is YOUR personal savior, you have the opportunity to mature and grow in your faith like never before!

I know that a lot of people aren't comfortable with change, but the truth is, everything is changing, literally! All things are either growing or dying, and there is nothing exempt from this fact. Heraclitus, a philosopher, says "you can never step in the same river twice." and I totally agree with that!

Once you place your foot in a river, the stream pattern changes; small dirt particles get washed away, changing the coarseness of your skin. If you were to put your foot in it again, it would be completely different. Change can't be avoided, so for me to say that your life is going to change, well, I'm just telling the truth! Even still, the change that I'm speaking of started because of the spiritual change that you've experienced.

The bible says that we go from *"children of darkness to children of the light"* (Ephesians 5:8). From being spiritually dead to being spiritually alive. When we make the decision to go from dark to light, there is a change that happens on the inside of us which can spark a change on our outside.

Being children of the light means that when you start your personal relationship with Jesus, you are literally crossing over from the kingdom of darkness to the kingdom of light. Think of it like this, you are a player on one sports team playing against another team. When you accept Jesus, it's like you are taking off your jersey and putting on a new one from the other team, the winning team! Also, this new team has been recruiting you ever since you started playing the game. They want to give you everything that you need to be the best player that you can be for them!

Hold on, let me encourage you real quick. This book isn't going to make you "JUST LIKE JESUS." I'm not going to guarantee that after reading this book, you will be the most powerful, faith-filled Christian ever to live, BUT! What this book will do is help you learn some basic principles that will guide you in your walk with The Lord.

So, if you're looking for a book to give you the secrets of being the best Christian ever, then you might want to pick up a different one, because this ain't it fam. But if you want to learn a few practical things that will help you grow in your relationship with God, then this book was made for you! I'm super excited to start this journey with you, so LET'S DO IT!!!

1

Your First Steps

First, YO! WELCOME TO THE FAMILY!!! It's always amazing to see brothers and sisters come to faith in the Lord and accept Jesus as their personal savior. I want you to know that I am HYPE about you making the decision to follow Jesus!

The Bible says in Luke 15:7, *"Heaven is rejoicing at the fact that you have made a decision to follow after Christ and to live for Him."* There is a party going on in heaven because you've just joined the fam, and now our family became bigger and stronger because you add so much value to it!

The decision that you've made to follow Jesus is the most amazing choice that you will ever make, and it will be an experience like none other. There won't be another decision in your life that will bring the amount of excitement and change like this one will.

It reminds me of an old movie called *The Matrix*, where the lead character Thomas Anderson had to make a *Major* decision about life after being sucked into an alternate world. He was offered to take a red pill or a blue pill. If he took the blue pill, his life would go back to normal, and he'd be accepting a life void of the truth. On the flip-side, if he took the red pill, then he would be exposed to the truth about the world, and his life would never be the same. [SPOILERS!] He decided to take the red pill, and his life changed forever!

Just like Thomas Anderson, you choosing to accept Jesus as your savior, now allows you to see the world differently. You'll be able to see who you are, and how you were made to impact the world.

This changes everything!

What Just Happened?!?

Jesus says, *"Your love for one another will prove to the world that you are my disciples"* (John 13:35). Now that you've chosen to follow Jesus, He is filling you with His love and you will begin to show God's love to other people. God sent Jesus as a sacrifice because He loves you and wants to have a relationship with you. This is the sacrifice that you accepted! Now, let me explain a bit more of how this happened.

God created Adam and Eve because He desires to be in relationship (Genesis 2:21-22). This relationship was fruitful and super beneficial, until sin came into the picture, and ruined everything! Adam disobeyed God when he did what God told him not to do. I mean he just flat out didn't listen to Him!

When that happened, sin entered the world, and it has affected every single human being, including you and me. The Bible says that *"all have sinned and fallen short of God's glory"* (Romans 3:23), and that we are *"Born in sin"* (Psalms 51:5). Or as Notorious B.I.G. put it, *"Born sinner, the opposite of a winner."*

God is Holy, meaning that He is without sin, and unless we are also holy, we cannot have a relationship with God. This is why Jesus is needed as a sacrifice. (Romans 6:23). The Bible says that *"The wages of sin is death..."*, which means that if you sin, you earn death. This death is not just a physical death, but it's also separation from God for eternity, like forever ever, forever ever, FOREVER EVER?! Yes, forever!

But [here comes the good news!], because Jesus lived a life without sin, He is able to have a relationship with God. Now that you have accepted Jesus as your own savior, He saves you by switching spots with you, and now God sees YOU the way He sees Jesus, without sin. Crazy right?!

God wants to have a relationship with YOU, and the only way for that to happen is by YOU choosing to accept Jesus as your personal savior. Now that you've done that, you have a personal relationship with Him, no ifs, ands, or buts! BOOM! That just happened!

What Does Being Saved Feel Like?

You may not know this, but you've just done something that is completely crazy... well, Crazy Awesome! Really, you have just changed the course of the future for you, your family, and your kids, and your kid's kids, and your kid's kid's ki...you get the point. Your life will never be the same, and not only will you change, you will also have an opportunity to change the world.
Now hold on a sec.

I know this may be a lot to take in all at once, and you might even feel a little overwhelmed, but I promise you it's all good. First off, let me make this clear, YOU. ARE. GOING. TO. CHANGE. PERIOD! No matter what, we as people change. We get older, some of us get wiser [and some of us don't, let's just be honest]. You most likely won't be the same person in a year because change is unavoidable.

Secondly, I want to encourage you to continue to trust God, because as you change, He'll be the one that will keep you on the right track. God will give you a deeper understanding of who He created you to be. So, as you continue this journey, starting with this crazy decision, you'll be able to look back and know that this was the best decision you've ever made.

At this point, you may not "feel" anything since you've chosen to follow Jesus, and I mean like, physically feel anything. I've heard amazing stories about people feeling the physical weight of their pain and burdens being lifted off them when they made the decision for follow Jesus, and some others say that they felt peace, a type of peace that they couldn't explain. These are great experiences for people, however these don't happen to everyone.

I've talked to a lot people that have said that when they made their decision to follow Christ, they felt good about it, but there was no "extraordinary feeling" that they felt. If you have an experience that is physically and emotionally ground breaking when you accept Jesus, great! That's not weird at all, but if you didn't have that kind of experience, that doesn't mean that you really aren't saved.

When I got saved, I was at a conference listening to a guy explain the gospel in simple terms. I sat in that auditorium listening, then I prayed and made my decision to follow Jesus. That was it. No physically groundbreaking experience, no overwhelming emotions. Just me choosing Jesus, and Him embracing me. You see, this experience is different for everyone, and you shouldn't compare your experience to someone else's. It's a trap! This comparison is dangerous because it can cause you to second guess the sincerity of your decision.

Don't Go Chasing Waterfalls

Now, I want to give you sort of a heads up about a few things you may experience now that you've decided to follow Christ. In 2nd Corinthians 5:17, Paul says that "anyone who belongs to Christ has become a new person. The old life is gone; a new life has begun!"

When you choose to follow Jesus, you'll notice that some people may not want to take that journey with you. You may see some people fade out of your life, some friends, maybe even some family. But Jesus said, *"And everyone who has left houses or brothers or sisters or father or mother or wife or children or fields for my sake will receive a hundred times as much and will inherit eternal life."* (Matthew 19:29)

You may also notice some of your desires and interest change, and there may be some things that you just start doing less. I had a friend in college that enjoyed drinking, a lot [and I ain't talking about no lemonade]. When she got saved, she started drinking less, and less, and less, until that desire was completely gone. Now, I'm not saying whether it is or isn't okay to drink alcohol, but what I am saying is that my friend had a desire that proved to be problematic and destructive for her. When she started to trust in the Lord, that problematic desire went away.

One thing that happens when you give your heart to God is that He'll teach you the desires of His heart, meaning He will allow you to feel what He feels about different things. When that happens, some of the other "feels" that you have, might fade away. But remember, "Don't go chasing waterfalls…" When people, and different desires start to fade away in your life, you may just have to let them go.

Sometimes you can even tell when it's time to do so. Don't chase them, don't run after them, just L.I.G.,

Let It Go. When you let them go, you make room for God to bring new people and new desires into your life. He will bring people that will love and challenge you to go deeper in your relationship with the Lord, and desires that will honor God while making you stronger in your walk with him.

What is a Christian, Exactly???

So let's switch gears a bit and talk about a few misconceptions when it comes to being a Christian. Hopefully this takes some of the pressure off.

1. Christians are not perfect, but we are being perfected.

This is one of the biggest struggles many Believers have. The idea that you must be perfect now that you are a Christian. WRONG! God never said that you MUST be perfect to be a Christian. In fact, God knows that you're going to mess up, eventually. That kind of sounds like a downer, but it's the truth. At some point you're going to try to do your own thing and disobey God. Remember what we just talked about, Romans 3:23, *"all have sinned and fallen short of God's glory"*, and when it says all, it means Err'body!

The book of Philippians makes it plain. It says in Chapter 2 verse 12, *"Work out your salvation with fear and trembling", or work out your salvation with respect, and recognize its importance."* The key here is "work it out"!

When I did a gym workout for the first time as a freshman in high school, I struggled! I could barely lift a 15-pound weight! I asked myself "Do you even lift Bro?!" Working out is hard, but the more you "work it out", you become more confident in your workouts, and you should be getting stronger. It's the same as a Believer, God doesn't expect you to do everything perfectly, but He wants you to work at it so that you can grow more confident and stronger as a Believer.

2. Sway ain't got all the answers, neither do all Christians.

All Believers are not encyclopedias, and they don't know everything about everything. There is a huge misconception that most Christians have the answers to life's toughest questions, but the truth is that we don't, and that's okay. You don't have to know everything there is to know about being a Christian right now, and I hope that you don't allow that pressure to get to you.

Yes, God wants us to learn and grow in our faith, just as it says in Proverbs 18:15, *"Wise men and women are always learning, always listening for fresh insights"* So as a Believer, you are encouraged to learn more and more about the Lord every day, but that doesn't mean that you have to know the answers to every biblical or moral question.

Let me give it to you straight. When people expect you to know everything about being a Christian, you feel the pressure to perfectly answer every question thrown at you. That's just not realistic fam. You don't have to know all the answers, and if you don't know the answer to something, ask someone who may be a bit more knowledgeable about the question being asked. Don't wing it and try to throw something together that may not be accurate. I've done that before, and it never works out too well.

A practical way of handling questions you don't know is by saying, "You know what, I don't know. But let's work together to figure out what the answer is." When you do this, it will either lead you to a more accurate answer to the question, or it'll expose the motive of the person asking the question.

After I got saved, one of my so-called friends asked me "I can drink alcohol, can't I? I mean, Jesus did turn water into wine, so He cool with it right?" I honestly didn't know the answer, I was still unsure about the whole drinking and being a Christian thing. I felt like if I said, "it's cool...", they would call me a hypocrite, or they'd say, "If Donte is a Christian and says it's cool, then God must be cool with it too!". On the other hand, if I said "naw fam...", they would call me lame, and say that being a Christian is lame. I felt stuck! Thankfully, I had a wiser friend who taught me how to say "I don't know" I told him that I didn't know the answer, and we could find out together. This exposed his heart, and he didn't want to talk about it anymore.

You see, this friend expected me to have an answer, which made me feel that pressure of being a perfect Christian and having all the right answers. I could've made something up just to look like I knew what I was talking about, but I learned that I didn't have to have the answer.

3. You can be a Christian and still have fun, right?

I've heard this so many times. "Oh, you're a Christian? Man, you must be bored all the time!". NOPE!

Not even close! Let me tell you, fun is not defined by what you do, but how and why you do it. For example, some people think football is fun because they enjoy the competition and excitement they get from it. There are people that feel that same way about chess. It's competitive, and you can get a lot of excitement from it! [trust me, I know, *as I adjust my thickly-framed glasses*].

Seriously though! You can have fun while being a Christian. [I'll let that sink in] You see, a lot people have an image in their mind of what fun looks like, and sometimes Christians don't quite fit into that. But let me say it again, it's not so much the "what" as it is the "how and why". The Bible says, *"Whatever you do in word or deed, do all in the name of the Lord Jesus, giving thanks through Him to God the Father."* (Colossians 3:17). So, when it comes to having fun, this simply means to honor God as you enjoy life. While you're enjoying the thrill of competition, or the laughter you share with your homies, remember the One who has given you the blessing of life and fun.

Growing

"So, how do I grow as a Christian?" This is a question that has been on the minds and in the hearts of Believers for years. Now I'm not claiming to have the ultimate answer for this question, but I'm convinced that we can grow in our faith by learning and practicing spiritual skills, like reading The Bible or praying.

This book is just one of many tools that can be used to help you grow in your faith and establish a firm foundation in your relationship with Jesus. Remember though, a tool is only good if it's being used, because if it's not being used, it's just as good as a brick in the ocean.

God's desire for you is that you grow into the man and woman that He has created you to be, one that is strong and full of courage. As you continue reading, I pray that you would take in what you're learning and put it into practice so that it helps you grow in your faith. James 2:26 says that *"For just as the body without the spirit is dead, so also faith without works is dead."*

You've taken a step of faith by accepting Jesus as your savior. Now it's time for you to follow that faith with some action. Now that you've accepted Jesus, let's walk together as you learn how to grow in your faith, so that you can become strong and courageous.

2

Assurance of Your Salvation

More Than Just a Prayer

So, tell me. Where were you when you made the decision to become a Christian? Were you sitting in church while someone up front spoke the truth about God, then invited you to begin a relationship with Jesus? Or were you talking one on one with someone and they started saying things that felt real to you?

For me, it was at a conference. The guy on stage shared the gospel in a way that made sense to me, and then... I prayed. That was it. You see, no matter where you were when it happened, I think it's safe to say that you started your relationship with God with a prayer.

I don't know about you, but after I prayed, I thought to myself, "is that it?" Even weeks after, there was still doubt in my mind about if I was really "saved" through that prayer. Well, I WAS saved through that prayer, and you were too. The truth we have to understand is that God hears us when we pray, and on a spiritual level, things happen when we pray.

When we pray to be saved, there is a spiritual change that happens, one that you may not "feel", but it does happen. Again, in Ephesians 5:8, it says *"For you were once darkness, but now you are light in the Lord. Live as children of light."* You go from being on the visiting team, to the being on the home team, literally! And spiritually!

[Major Key!] We go from being in the darkness [Satan's team], to being in the light [God's team], and all of that happened when we prayed that prayer of salvation. This may have seemed like a simple prayer, but it's a really huge deal! One that changed the game up!

Three Stages of Salvation

When you are saved, you have received salvation. Now, within the process of salvation, there are three stages. Let me break this down like a car with no gas. The three stages of salvation are justification, sanctification, and glorification. Don't let me lose you now. Big words make me nervous too, but let's chop it up like a salad.

I think it's safe to say that the most talked about stage of these three is the first stage, justification. My man Webster says that justification means "the act of judging, regarding, or treating as righteous and worthy" For the Christian, it means "being regarded and treated as righteous in the eyes of God."

This is the stage that happened when you said that small but powerful prayer, "God I'm a sinner, and I need to be saved from my sin. I believe that Jesus died for me so that I can be saved, and I accept Him as my savior right now" and BOOYAH! That's it! We are now justified by God, through Jesus. Because Jesus is our savior, God now sees us the same way He sees Jesus, justified.

Immediately after justification is Sanctification. Say it with me, Sank-Tah-Fih-Kay-Shun. Got it? Good. All this means is "to set apart", that's it. Well, technically it means "to set apart to a sacred purpose or to religious use", but we'll go with the first one. Sanctification is a process that starts because of salvation and lasts throughout your entire journey as a Christian on this earth.

When you accept Jesus, God begins to change you, and set you apart. He's causing you to look, act, and even think differently than the rest of the world. God wants you to become holy, or simply put, be more like Him in your thoughts and actions. Now I'm not saying that you have to be this "super-weird Jesus lover person" like you see in movies. You know, the one claiming to be better than other people and all. What I will say is, when you live the way God desires you to live, it's going to look a little different than how the rest of the world lives.

The last stage is glorification. We won't spend too much time on this one because it's something that happens when you get to heaven, and, well, let's just say that this topic can get pretty deep.

Right now, our physical bodies aren't made to last forever. Along with that, our human nature limits us in many ways, and we also make all kinds of mistakes. When we pass away and go to heaven, our bodies will become brand spanking new! No more headaches, diseases, or anything else that causes us pain. Also, sin will be completely removed from us, and we will be made perfect in that way.

In short, glorification is when God changes you for His good, and for good. That's about all we need to know for now.

Finally, all of these stages are possible because of the Holy Spirit. He is the one who leads you to accept Christ, He is the one who sanctifies you, and the one that leads us to the process of glorification. We'll learn a bit more about the Holy spirit in the next chapter, but let's move on to some of the common misconceptions of salvation. *cues 80's break dancing music*

Common Misconceptions About Salvation

Many people believe that a salvation is supposed to look a certain way. The problem is that people have their own individual ideas of what salvation is, and that creates many major misconceptions about the process.

Here are a few of them.

"You can only be saved after you turn age __**__": Wrong yo. It doesn't matter what age you are. As long as you understand who Jesus is, why he died, and you accept Him as your savior.

"I'm saved because my grandma prays for me": Nope! Only YOU can accept Jesus as YOUR savior, you can't do it for anyone else, and they can't do it for you.

"I prayed the prayer, and I'm saved. Now I can do whatever I want!": Nada! Read the section you just read about sanctification and please tell me if that makes sense, then go read Romans 6:1. If you believe and confess, great! That's stage one. Now on to stage two. Keep on keepin' on.

"I feel bad for my mistakes, and I'm sorry Jesus. Amen.": Okaaaaay... ? I'm glad you see the error in your ways, but, it's not just about feeling bad.

"I'm saved because I'm a good person": Say what?! Jesus said, *"I am the way, and the truth, and the life; no one comes to the Father but through Me."* (John 14:6) That means, you can only be saved through Jesus, that's it. Doing good is... good, but it's not what salvation is.

How Do You Know That You Know?

Believe it or not, there are many people that have many different opinions about when you are "officially saved", or when you can know without a shout of a doubt that you are saved! I don't claim to be a theologian or some deep thinker, but I just don't think it's as deep as some people make it out to be. I believe that one verifiable way to know that you know that you are saved is by the change that happens in your life.

If you are saved [like you actually believe and confess] there will be a change that happens in your life. That change may not happen fast, but it will happen. In 1st Corinthians 3, Paul talks about having to "feed" the Believers truth like milk for babies, because they were not ready for "solid foods" yet. He's saying that it's a process. So yes, your life will begin to look differently, your thoughts, and maybe even your actions.

You will know that you are saved by seeing the transformation of your heart over time. I know, it's not an easy answer, sort of like that old question "How do I know that I'm in love?" Well, this ain't no love book homie, but as a Believer, you better believe that salvation brings about change, and that change will be noticeable in time. Just hang on tight.

It's a process homie.

3

The Holy Spirit, who dis?

"The Holy Spirit...ummm?" *blank stare* Yeah, this is usually what happens when I mention the Holy Spirit or reference Him [yes, Him]. There's so much to talk about when it comes to the Holy Spirit, especially as a new Believer. A lot of people haven't been taught or haven't really heard much about Him. Let me give you a few key points about this, ready...?

The Holy Spirit is God, the third part to the Trinity. *What's the Trinity?* It's the combination or makeup of God, in His entirety. You have God the Father, which is who we usually refer to as just God. You have God the Son, which we typically call Jesus, who was all God and all man [let that blow your mind in 3..2...1, POW!].

The best example I can think of to describe this is, think of a man who is a son and a father to his own children. He is fully both, and never not one or the other. Lastly, you have the Holy Spirit, which I think is like the brother that is just as strong as his other brothers, but people forget about Him.

1st Corinthians 2:10 helps us know that the Holy Spirit is God, but there can be such a misunderstanding of who He is that His role sort of gets swept under the rug. So, let's check out a few of the roles that the Holy Spirit fills in our lives as Believers. We're going to focus on a few of the things that the Holy Spirit gives us, which will help us define who He is and what He does.

The Holy Spirit Gives Power

Being a Christian is hard. In fact, it's impossible to be a Christian, at least without help from God. That help for us is the Holy Spirit. Jesus said it, so I believe it (John 15:16-17). One thing that the Holy Spirit gives us is power. The Holy Spirit gives us power, and it's that power that keeps us from not going crazy as a Christian.

Power to live differently

The Holy Spirit gives us power to live differently than the world around us. It's very easy to do what everyone else is doing, but it takes power to be different. As people, we naturally look out for ourselves, and look to benefit ourselves by any means necessary; just think about little kids! You don't have to teach them how to lie, or how to be sneaky. When I was 6, I used to sneak cookies to my room and hide them under my pillow, just so I could eat them when it was time to go to bed, even though my dad told me not to. [yeah, cookies. Don't judge me.]

This is our true nature as humans, selfish. Jeremiah 17:9 says *"Nothing can hide its evil as well as the human mind. It can be very sick, and no one really understands it."* This means that we as people can, and possibly will do whatever we have to, so that we can get what we want, even if someone else gets hurt in the process. The Holy Spirit is the one that gives us the power us to live differently and to overcome this selfishness.

Now I know, our parents and role models teach us morals and values so that we can be decent human beings, but it's deeper than that. In our hearts, and left up to us, we would live a life that would be all about us. God's desire is that we live differently, and not how the rest of the world lives. God wants us to model our lives after Jesus, and the only way for us to even start that process, is through the power of the Holy Spirit.

Power to make wise decisions and beat temptation

Again, we as people, naturally want what we want, when we want it, and how we want it, but life ain't a giant Burger King! The problem we run into often is that we want things that aren't always bad for us, but the way we go after those things can be bad. Sometimes we are so tempted to get what we want right now that we don't stop to think "I wonder what God thinks about this?"

Just look at Abraham and Sarai in Genesis 16. They wanted a kid and weren't able to have one when they wanted to, so instead of talking to God about it, they took matters into their own hands, and it got messy, fast!

This is where the Holy Spirit comes in, acting as a guide for us. He taps us on the shoulder when we are about to do something stupid [I've had that happen plenty of times]. The Holy Spirit gives us power to overcome the temptation to do what might not be best, and He helps lead us to making better decisions.

Power to spread the Good News about Jesus

The Holy Spirit also give us power to share the good news about God and Jesus to other people, so that they can experience God for themselves. For me, when it comes to talking to people about God, a lot of times I just feel like I don't know what to say.

In these moments, the Holy Spirit gives me power and confidence to just talk about what God has done in my life. This usually leads to an amazing conversation and a seed being planted in someone's heart to start thinking about God. This all starts with the power from the Holy Spirit.

Luke 12:11-12 says *"When they bring you before the synagogues and the rulers and the authorities, do not be anxious about how you should defend yourself or what you should say, for the Holy Spirit will teach you in that very hour what you ought to say."* Sometimes we get nervous about talking to other people about God, but we can rest easy knowing that the Holy Spirit will give us the power we need to share about God.

Activation

So, the Holy Spirit gives you this power to live differently, to make wise decisions, and power to spread the good news about Jesus. I think one big question that gets asked is "How do I know that I have this power?" or "When did I get this power?" The short answer is, you gain access to this power when you get saved. The moment you accept Jesus as your savior, you gain access to this power that the Holy Spirit gives.

However, there's one small piece that gets missed by a lot of people, you have to activate this power from the Holy Spirit. It's like when you get a new phone. It's all ready to work, it's nice, shiny, and brand new. However, in order to get service, you have to call your phone company and have them activate it! Let me tell you that the Holy Spirit is ready to give you power to live, but you have to activate that power!

The way you activate this Holy Spirit power is through prayer. Say what?! Yeah man, the way you gain this power that Holy Spirit has is by asking God for it. Truth is, He really wants you to have it! Jesus tells us in Luke 11:9-13, *"So I say to you: Ask and it will be given to you; seek and you will find; knock and the door will be opened to you. For everyone who asks receives; the one who seeks finds; and to the one who knocks, the door will be opened. "Which of you fathers, if your son asks for a fish, will give him a snake instead? Or if he asks for an egg, will give him a scorpion? If you then, though you are evil, know how to give good gifts to your children, how much more will your Father in heaven give the Holy Spirit to those who ask him!"*

It's like you have the keys to a super dope car, and you're sitting in the driver's seat with the keys in your hand, you now have the option to sit there with the key thinking about how great this car is, or you can put the keys in the ignition, and start the car and really enjoy it!

Long story short, you must ask for this power, and if you really, really want it, it's easy. Pray this, "God, I believe that You are God, Father, Son, and Holy Spirit, and I want to have the power of the Holy Spirit so that I can live differently, beat temptation, and share the good news about Jesus. Lord You said if I ask for it, I will receive it, so I'm asking for it, and believe that you will give me that power right now in Jesus name I pray, Amen."

There you go homie, now keep praying this consistently, and watch God work!

Fruit of the Holy Spirit

When we ask for the power of the Holy Spirit and receive it, we also get the fruit of the spirit. We find these in Galatians 5:22-23 *"But the fruit of the Spirit is love, joy, peace, patience, kindness, goodness, faithfulness, gentleness, self-control;"* The fruit of the spirit are characteristics of God that we're able to imitate, causing us to live more and more like Jesus. These characteristics not only are placed inside of us, but they also help guide us in our journey as Believers.

Now, when it comes to this fruit, our goal is to produce this fruit, like a tree does. We can pray to receive the Holy Spirit, and just like that we can receive Him. However, in order to produce the fruit of the Spirit, we have to put in a little work. For example, we can pray for patience, but the funny thing that God does sometimes, is that He won't just give us patience like "BWAM!" Now you're the most patient person ever.

He puts us in scenarios where we have to work on being patient. Think about that the next time you are driving behind someone going two miles an hour under the speed limit. Allow your patience to be developed, along with the other fruits of the Spirit.

Gifts Given From the Holy Spirit

The Holy Spirit is a gift in and of Himself, just like Jesus said in Luke 11. The Holy Spirit also brings gifts He wants to give us so that we can become strong and effective Christians. This will help us in loving God, loving people, and changing the world. God is super eager to give us these gifts, and all we have to do is ask for them. It's just like when we asked for the power of the Holy Spirit, we can ask for these gifts which are all different and powerful.

I want to introduce you to them so that you know that you have access to these gifts, but I encourage you to talk to your local pastor or mentor about them more in depth.

Just to name a few that are found in 1st Corinthians 12, one gift the Holy Spirit can give us the gift of healing, and I mean like real, physical healing! This is like being able to help people heal like Wolverine, except without the claws and that hair.

Another gift the Holy Spirit wants to give us is the gift of Wisdom. The wisdom I'm talking about is like Master Roshi with the Teenage Mutant Ninja Turtles type of wisdom. The difference though, is that this wisdom from the Holy Spirit is truly divine. It's a gift that will help you love God more, love people more, and even more so, change the world. These are just a few of the Gifts that the Holy Spirit wants to give, and yes you have access to them all.

Here are a few more gifts of the Holy Spirit:

Gift of Service

Gift of Hospitality

Gift of Speaking in Tongues

Gift of Interpreting the Speaking in Tongues

Gift of Discernment

Gift of Prophesy

Gift of Faith

4

Grow Up!

The Holy Spirit no doubt gives you power to live differently and boldly in your faith, and you now know that it's the Holy Spirit that helps you grow. Now, we will talk about growth as a Believer. We're going to focus on what you can do practically to help you grow in your faith.

Why is Growth Important

"Why should I worry about growing???" Well, I'm glad you asked. There's this idea out there that once you get saved, you're set! You're getting into Heaven, and there is nothing else that you have to do as a Christian. Just don't kill anyone, and you're good, right…? WRONG! It only starts there, remember when we talked about that little thing called Sank-Tah-Fih-Kay-Shun? This is what growth is. Now, let me tell you why we need growth.

Many people believe that if you're not growing, you're dying. I want to switch that up and tell you that "In life, you are always growing, but in what?" I think that we as people are always growing. Whether it's growing in wisdom, or growing in recklessness; growing in joy, or growing in pain. Growth cannot be avoided, good and bad. You can be growing taller, or growing older, it's still a form of growth.

With that said, there are some areas in our lives where we can choose if and how we grow, and as Believers, I think it's important to choose to grow in our faith. Peter tells us in 1st Peter 2:2, *"Like newborn babies, crave pure spiritual milk, so that by it you may grow up in your salvation"* So, I think it's safe to say that God wants us to grow in our faith.

What Growth Looks Like to the Believer

When I became a Believer, I was pretty set on the idea that there was one type of growth that existed for Believers, "fast growth". Now, the longer that I've been saved, the more I understand that growth is not about how fast or how much, but about how long. As a Christian, it's all about the long game, because it really is a marathon.

I hate long distance running! I mean I really despise it. However, I know that there are a lot of benefits that I can get from it. When it comes to long distance running, the one thing that I always remember is that even though having good pace and good technique is beneficial, the major key is that you actually put one foot in front of the other and move forward.

Practical ways on How to Grow

Let's just jump right into some of the practical ways that you're able to grow as a Believer.

1. Read the Bible

I cannot tell you how many times I've been asked "How do I grow in my faith?" and when I respond "Fam, read your Bible.", folks are thrown off. Most times it's because they were expecting some deep theological or philosophical answer. This honestly is the simplest and maybe the most practical answer that I can give, and there are two reasons why I say this.

Reason one, the Bible is LITERALLY God's word. Meaning that these are the words that He wanted us to read and learn from. God's not pulling any punches. What better way to grow in our relationship with God than to read the book that He specifically wrote for us? [That makes sense to me]

Secondly, you can apply what you learn from the Bible immediately. When the Bible says, *"...but let everyone be quick to listen and slow to speak and slow to anger."* (James 1:19), you can do that with the very next person you talk to! There are so many practical teachings that will help you grow in your faith as you learn and apply them.

2. Pray

Believe it or not, prayer is a great way to grow in our faith and in our relationship with God. Simply put, prayer is when we communicate, or talk to God. With that said, I'll also say that prayer can seem interesting at times. I know that prayer is a very effective way to grow in our faith, but sometimes it can seem mysterious to us. Part of that is because prayer is not a formula or equation, and also, it's not something you do where you see immediate growth, like "Expecto Patronum", and boom! [nerd moment! just goggle Harry Potter if you don't get that]

Many people think they have an idea of what prayer looks like, but to be honest, a lot of us have it wrong. We sometimes view prayer as this boring time where we have to come up with the perfect words to say to God. This is so NOT true. We also believe that if we pray for something that doesn't happen right away, our prayers don't work, but that's not right either.

While I was a counselor at a summer camp called Kids Across America, there was a period where my voice was completely gone for about a week. This become frustrating because we were encouraged to cheer and yell when we were excited, but I couldn't. I prayed for my voice to come back quickly, but it didn't for a while. Even though it took time for my voice to come back, it was through these times of prayer that I learned how to be patient and how to trust God's timing. This was a major time of growth for me.

When it comes to prayer, I think that there are three things you should understand about prayer so that you can have a proper view of it.

Prayer is simple.

Prayer is you talking to God about what is on your mind, just like a conversation with your friends… [sort of] When you boil down prayer, you get to a place where your words don't have to be perfect, God knows what you are trying to say, but He still wants to communicate with you.

Prayer is a discipline.

It's something that you should do consistently, whether you see your growth right away or not. Trust me, when you start praying consistently, you are growing. You may not see it right away, but you are. It can be hard at times, but that's why you have to be disciplined. Find a time and a place where you can talk to God consistently. It doesn't matter if it's for 5 minutes or 5 hours. When you do this consistently, you will begin to see yourself grow.

Prayer is connecting

Remember that prayer is a time where you connect with God. It's not a time to make a wish list for God, nor is it a time to make up this elaborate production to perform, it's just time with God.

Prayer is a MAJOR KEY in your growth as a Believer. Remember that when we have a good view of what prayer is, we can do it and see growth over time. One of my favorite books is a little book called *Prayers That Availeth Much,* by Word Ministries Inc., it's my go to when it comes to praying bible-based prayers.

That sort of wraps up these few pointes on prayer, lets move on.

3. Community

I remember in the 4th grade, in my music class we sang a song called "It Take a Village to Raise a Child". As a youngster I had no idea what that meant! Now that I'm older, and just a little bit wiser, I've come to understand this statement. I've also learned that in the same way a village raises a child, a community is what sustains an individual.

It takes more than just your perspective to help you grow in your faith. In order to grow you need some people who are like-minded, but also others who think a little differently than you. These folks can give you a new perspective and foster growth in your walk with Jesus.

Too often I see Believers trying to be "Lone Rangers", when God calls us to be a Tribe. Community is when you allow Believers you trust into your life and spend time with them. You start to develop relationships with them while also sharing your joys and sorrows with them.

By simply surrounding yourself with these folks, who are also growing in their relationships with God, you will see growth in your own walk. Just a little reminder, most times when someone stops growing in their relationship with God, one reason is because they are disconnected from their community. Keep an eye out for the people in your community, stay connected with them so that you all can keep growing together.

4. Volunteer

"I love volunteering to help the less fortunate. It makes you feel all tingly inside!" When I hear this statement, I don't know if I want to clap for this person, or karate chop them in the neck!

There's great benefit in helping people and volunteering your time, but there are many times where people do it so that they can say that they're a good person. I think that if you volunteer or help others, it should change you; it should cause you to think about why you're doing it and cause you to grow from it. We are to look out for those who are in need and show them God's love. (James 1:27)

Helping people that are in need is an amazing way to grow in your faith. Not only does it expose you to what others may need, but it can also make you very thankful for what and who you have in your life. When you volunteer for something, it should be done so that you can share the love of God with others while being an example for others.

Let me add though, as good as volunteering may be, you have to check your motives and be sure you don't have some kind of expectation to gain something. This process of checking your motives is another way that you can grow, because it forces you to be honest with yourself. When you volunteer in a way that shows God's love, you get a chance to grow in your own walk with God.

5. Mentoring/Discipleship

In the New Testament of the Bible it talks about the 12 Disciples. 12 Dudes that walked with Jesus while He was on earth. On the surface we see them as followers, but when you look deeper, you see that these 12 guys got a chance to watch Jesus share God's love, help people in need, and see Him be a friend to many.

This is discipleship; letting someone, or you watching someone live their life as they pursue God and grow. This is one of the most potent ways to grow, because you are 1-on-1, or in a small group, and you have immediate access to a mature Believer's life

As a new Believer, I think that it is SUPER important to be around mature Believers. It's also beneficial to find one that you can either trust, or learn to trust, and ask them to mentor you. Bottom line, you are learning how to be a Christian, and what better way to do this than to learn by having someone help you and guide you as you grow!? I mean, that makes sense to me *bruh bruh*! If I want to be a great singer, I could take lessons, but along with that, how much more would I benefit from learning from someone who's already great at it???

As we grow in our faith, remember that there is someone behind us trying to grow in their faith as well. They too, are looking for someone to mentor them that is a mature believer. When you become mature [which, you just know when you know, and when others can see that maturity], it's your turn to mentor someone.

To take the pressure off a little, as a mature Believer, the only formula[ish] to mentoring is to share your life with that person; everything else is extra. It's not having all the answers or being able to systematically exegete the whole Bible. It's being able to help someone grow in their faith, while still growing in yours. If you're not ready to do that, it's okay, take your time to mature and grow. Just remember that this is something that Jesus calls us to do when we are mature.

These are just a few examples of things you can do that will help you grow in your faith. I really want to encourage you to start putting these things into practice.

James 1:22 – *"Do what God's teaching says; when you only listen and do nothing, you are fooling yourselves."*

Stay humble, stay hungry.

5

Zeal vs. Excitement

Victory!

"Yo! You just got saved!! [or you've been for a little bit now] Maybe you've told some of your family, your friends, or even some random people!!! Let's throw a party! Oh, and to make your salvation officially official, let's get you involved in every program we can, get you to give your story of how you got saved, let's volunteer, mentor, get mentored, play on the church music team, do 3 bible studies a week, and a prayer night! All while still trying to juggle your already challenging life! Right?!?"

WRONG!!!

Well, ok. This is a snapshot of what my life looked like when I first got saved. I was in college, studying to become an engineer [we'll talk about that another time]. I got saved in October of that year and got super involved. For me, this was kind of a mistake because I began to get overwhelmed with my responsibilities. Even though I grew in my faith, I started to fail in many other areas of my life.

"What's wrong with that?! I mean, isn't growing in your faith the most important thing in your life, by any means?"

Yes and no. You see, the Bible says that *"in everything that we do, do it in the name of Jesus"* (Colossians 3:17), meaning that we should do everything in a way that brings glory to God while also doing it with excellence.

As I was dead smack in the middle of my undergraduate career, I struggled to maintain a 2.3 gpa, and remain active in about 10 organizations. I heard a young lady say something that shook me up and straighten me out about what I should be focusing on. She said "I have a 4.0, and I'm involved in 2 organizations. Second to being a Christian, my main obligation here is to be a student. God has blessed me with this opportunity to glorify Him with my academics and studies."

SMACK! Right up side my head

Zeal vs Excitement

When we get saved, sometimes there is a level of excitement that gets stirred up in us, and we feel as if we can do anything and everything! We are so excited to tell people about Jesus, to get involved, and to do all these "Christian things", but let's just slow down for a quick second and breeeeaaathe. Wooosaahh... Okay, let's talk about the difference between excitement and zeal.

I think many of us know what it means to be excited, but if not, let me refresh your memory. To be excited is to be eager or enthusiastic about something, being full of joy or thrilled by something. *"Okay, now what's zeal?"* Well I'm glad you asked! Zeal is to be eager or enthusiastic while pursuing a goal or having a cause [you see where I'm going with this].

The difference between the two is that excitement is typically an emotional response to something, and at some point, it fades away. Zeal on the other hand, is a long-standing passion that involves devotion and a long-term focus.

Let's take it a little further, Excitement is a short sprint and zeal is a marathon. Both can be beneficial, but our walk with God is a marathon, not a sprint. Excitement can cause you to think in and for the moment, making decisions that may feel good right now while not taking into account the big picture.

Excitement is going to the store and putting everything you want into a cart without counting how much money you have. Excitement is getting involved in as much as you can without really thinking about how it all will help you and how you can balance it all.

On the other hand, zeal is taking a step back and thinking about your long-term goals. Zeal is planning a long road trip, and mapping out your stops, and counting the cost of it all. Are you picking up what I'm laying down? We must remember that our walk with God is a long race, and the goal is to be consistent. Having just excitement can cause you to go up and down too often, and only focus on what's fun or what gives you a thrill in the moment. Zeal will help you to be level and to move forward consistently, not doing things just to do them.

"I HAVE to Do This!"

Sometimes we try to overcompensate or make up for lost time.

We get saved, right? And how we move forward from that point is so important because it begins to lay the foundation of our faith. I'm thankful that while still young in my faith, someone taught me the difference between excitement and zeal, and I became aware of the areas in my life where I was operating with only excitement and no zeal.

Let me say it again, excitement can be good, but if that's all you have, then you could be lacking a long-term view of your Christian walk. Also, you could become easily sidetracked or overwhelmed with where you are in life.

I've seen a lot of people get saved, then jump head first into so many things, trying to rush their growth as a Believer. Most of the time this resulted in them becoming overwhelmed and quitting many things. What happens sometimes is we get saved, and we start to think in the short-term, "what's good for me today and right now" and not consider "what's good for me now that will also carry me over the next year, or 5 years."

This is why it's important to understand excitement vs zeal, because if all you have is excitement for the now, then it could create the expectation that every minute of your Christian life will be filled with thrill and pleasure. This thinking can cause you to become frustrated when things are "regular", or even when life gets hard.

The truth is that life can and will be hard at times, and so will your walk with God. However, when you are focused on your long-term walk with God, it's your zeal for God that will get you through those times and teach you how to be consistent.

How to Increase Zeal

So if zeal is so important to have, how do I get it?

And how do I keep it?

As a good friend of mine used to say, "Let me learn'ya something!" Obtaining and keeping your zeal for God is totally possible! You have to know that it is more of a practice than anything. There are a few practical things that you can do to help, some are similar to what we discussed in Chapter 4: Grow Up!.

1. Make time

Carve out a set time every day to spend with God, reading the Bible and praying. This will help create consistency for you and for your relationship with God. This will also help in disciplining yourself to think about things that will foster long-term growth in your Christian life.

2. Get a Mentor

Find a mentor that you are able to learn from and ask questions. Paul of the Bible, you know the guy that wrote like half of the New Testament, not only studied about God before He came to know Jesus, but He also studied with a guy named Barnabas. He did this for quite some time before he started his own ministry (Acts 13:1-3). In essence, it's great to have a mentor or someone you can go to that will help you better understand your walk with the Lord and create a firm foundation in your faith.

3. Be Human

I mean really, remember that you are a human, not a machine. Remember that you have limits, and that you need time to rest and rejuvenate from the things that you involve yourself in. Every runner doesn't run in every single race they get invited to, right? I'm not saying take a break from being a Christian every once and awhile, but what I am saying is try not to over commit to things and fill your schedule up so much that you begin to fail or struggle. It's like what one of my mentors taught me, you can either be mediocre in a lot of things or be great in a few things.

Now I know that there are going to be times in your life where things are just crazy busy and there's no way around them. It happens. Remember though, as you grow in your zeal for God, be careful that you don't let your pure excitement lead you into doing and committing to things that could, over time, cause you to burn out and quit. You are in a marathon, not a sprint, and you don't have to feel obligated to participate in every single thing that seems good.

Pace yourself.

6

Community

"Friends.... How many of us have them?!"

Really? Friends are hard to come by, and it becomes a bit harder when you begin to put standards on the type of friends that you are looking to have. Your friends and the community that you surround yourself with are incredibly important, especially when it comes to growing in your faith.

One of my mentors used to say, "show me your friends and I'll show you your future". I know that this is true, however I believe that on a bigger scale, your community, the larger culture of people that you are around, have a greater impact on your life and your faith. I say this because I believe that your friends are like your siblings, except you get to pick them. Your community is like your siblings, parents, aunts and uncles, cousins, and so on. They are the larger group of people that you find yourself around that affect you directly and indirectly.

Let me be clear, your friends will come from your community, but just as you can determine who your friends are, you have the choice to decide what your community looks like. Friends can bring so much value to your life, but your community brings more to your table, giving you many different perspectives, resources, and more opportunities to see life being lived out by different people.

The Righteous and The Ratchet

When we look at Paul in the bible, we see that before he was a Believer (Acts 9), his community consisted of people who were super political. They looked down on other people, and for the most part, they were just ratchet all around. In Acts chapter 6 and 7, we see these so-called religious dudes, not only challenging the disciple Stephen, but also lying about Stephen so that they could take the law into their own hands and kill him.

Among these crazy fools, was Paul. You see, this is what Paul's community consisted of, and because these were the people that he surrounded himself with, Paul acted like them, spoke like them, and thought like them. It wasn't until Paul got radically saved, in Acts chapter 9, that He began to change his community. This lead to Him growing in his faith and living a life that became a great example for Christians all over the world.

Paul's new community taught him how to love people like Jesus and how to grow strong in his faith. Just as Paul's community helped him in his walk with the Lord, your community can do the same, if you allow them to.

What a Life-Giving Community Looks Like

Before I got saved, my friends and my community seemed…. Normal I guess. I had friends that I joked around with, we hung out a lot, and we also had a lot of deep conversations about life and our futures. I know that my community wasn't bad [bad], but looking back, I know that many of the people that I surrounded myself with weren't looking to the Lord for direction. None of us were looking to the Creator and asking about why we were created.

Yes, we did things that were good for the local community and for others, but there was no real direction. On top of that, most of us had no real purpose. At this point, I began to question what my community looked like, because when you are in a community that has no purpose, you could end up anywhere and everywhere except for the place that you think you want to be.

One thing I learned [and it took me a while to learn] was that it's important to surround yourself with a community of people that are life-giving. *WAIT!!! What you do mean life-giving???* My bad, let me explain, when I say life-giving community, I mean being around people that love you, that encourage you, and that give you biblical truth that you can use in your everyday life.

Proverbs 18:21 says *"Words kill, words give life; they're either poison or fruit—you choose."* So, when you are encouraging and loving the way Jesus does, and speak words of support and truth in a Godly way, that can be defined as giving life. As you are forming your community, you want to make sure that you have a lot of people that are life-giving, because these will be the people that'll help you grow in your faith and support you in your walk with God.

Choosing a Llife-Giving Community

So now that you know what a life-giving community does, let's figure out how to choose a life-giving community. This could seem a little overwhelming when you think of having to choose fifty-plus people that you are going to surround yourself with constantly, but let's look at it and I'll break it down for you like a Break Dancer and a cardboard box.

A community is made up of the larger group and culture of people that you are around consistently, down to your closest friends that you see every day. When you are looking to define your community, think about your job and the people there as a part of your community. You can include your school and the folks you may study with as a part of your community. Your local church is also a part of your community.

With that, you can think about getting involved in small groups, which is a smaller community of people [about 3-12 people]. I'd suggest meeting with these folks frequently with the intention of making friendships with them. It's here that you'll have the opportunity to talk about your faith, life, and other joys and struggles that you encounter.

Like I said earlier, your friends, the closest people to you, are the ones that could really impact you the most. When you are you looking for friends, find ones that are Believers, that are inspiring, but also ones that are truthful with you and don't pull any punches.

Choosing Friends

The friends that you choose can lead to a very prosperous and enjoyable future. On the flip side, you can also choose people that make you sad and want to sit in a dark room and listen to "Everybody Hurts" on repeat while eating ice cream. [Well, the ice cream part doesn't sound too bad]

When you are choosing friends, you want to make sure that they are individuals that you not only connect well with, but also ones that are ride or die! I mean, friends that will walk this Christian walk with you for the rest of your lives, encouraging you and helping you be who God has called you to be. You also want to make sure that your friends keep you accountable and talk to you in love and grace (John 13:34-35).

Your friends can and should be a bit different from you. If all your friends are exactly like you, then you may want to expand your community [I'm just saying]. Having friends that are different lets you have people close to you that have different perspectives. This is SUPER beneficial because it can make you think about things in a different light or from a different angle.

I really don't know of any other criteria that you can have when choosing your friends, except, you will just know. You'll know if they are good for you or not when you honestly look at yourself and whether your relationship with God is growing. To have amazing friends that are Believers is a blessing, and I really want you to find those homies that will be like siblings, or closer.

Choosing a Church

Now, let's look at the larger group of people that you are around, and when I say larger group, I'm really talking about your church family. Honestly, choosing a church can be difficult, mainly because churches, just like anything else, are filled with imperfect people.

I think it's really important to remember that churches are meant to be a place for broken people to go to, so that God can heal them. When you are looking for a church, try not to look for the perfect church with perfect people, because you probably won't find one. However, when you are looking for a church, consider having 3 levels of criteria; Needs, wants, and preferences.

Needs

Here are a few examples of what <u>needs</u> you could have for a church:

1. Your church **NEEDS** to be a bible-led, bible preaching church. This means that all of their messages are rooted in the bible and their programs are aimed at filling a biblical need or mandate.

2. Your church **NEEDS** to meet regularly. We can only grow as Believers if we are consistently and regularly engaged in God's things, and this is no different. Make sure there are regular meetings, preferably weekly.

3. Your church **NEEDS** to be life-giving. When you are looking for your church, make sure they are life-giving. The best example I can think of is a church of people that loves you like 1 Corinthians 13:4-7, *"Love is patient, love is kind. It does not envy, it does not boast, it is not proud. It does not dishonor others, it is not self-seeking, it is not easily angered, it keeps no record of wrongs. Love does not delight in evil but rejoices with the truth. It always protects, always trusts, always hopes, always perseveres"*.

Wants

When it comes to wants, these are things that you want your church to have but aren't necessarily deal-breakers like "needs". These are important things that you want at your church. Here are a few examples:

1. You **WANT** a church with an active youth group. Especially if you have kids, you may want a church that also has a place where youngsters can grow in their faith and be exposed to other Believers.

2. You **WANT** a church that has many options for small group meetings. This would give you a chance to find people that are interested in some of the same things you are. We know we all [or most folks] want to grow in their faith, but it would also be nice to know Believers that like to knit, or play baseball, or read books just like you.

3. You **WANT** a church that emphasizes on evangelism or missions. This is a want, a church that shares your heart on certain biblical things, but still recognizing the larger picture, that all Believers in the world are united by Jesus. Again, these are things that are important to you.

Preferences

Simply put, preferences are things that you prefer. If the church has them, great! If not, well, you can be okay without them. Here are a few examples:

1. You **PREFER** a church that uses more technology and gives you easy access to information.

2. You **PREFER** a church that is within 20 miles of where you live.

3. You **PREFER** a church that dresses more casual, like jeans and t-shirt, so that you're a little more comfortable. Also, you can bring friends without them worrying about how they look.

You can make these criteria look however you want, but my advice is that you connect with a few Believers that you trust and see what churches they are going to and check them out. Be open but try not to assume that every church is supposed to be perfect, and if one thing on your "wants" and "preferences" list isn't there, don't write it off completely.

Also, a few added notes. When you visit a new church, go early and stick around after its done. See how people interact and look to meet a few folks. If you've been going to a church for a few weeks and like it, think of any questions you have about the church, the bible, or just life, and set up a meeting with the pastor of the church to hear their perspective on your questions. And lastly, pray about it. Let God lead you. He'll draw your heart to a place where you feel like "this is right".

Let Me Tell You Why

Your life-giving community will have many people that will show you love, support, and perspective. Remember, you are able to choose your community. There will be people that will come into your life that add value to you, but there will also be some folks that you'll have to cut ties with or separate yourself from. I can't lie, this can be a hard process, but it's necessary.

My encouragement to you is this, focus on God, grow in your faith, and keep the friends and community members that support you close. The folks that are always challenging who you are now, and what you believe; those that pressure to you or do things that just don't sit right with you anymore, you may need to slowly distance yourself from them.

Don't get me wrong, there are many relationships that will have value that may not fit this sort of mold, and I'm not saying get rid of them. What I am saying is, be mindful of the people you are influencing, but also be mindful of the people that you are influencing.

Give Life.

7

Quiet Time, Devo. Whatever You Call It

"We got to pray, just to make it today" ~MC Hammer

Years ago, my wife told me "You can either worry, or you can pray, but you can't do both!" When she said this, it hit me square in the nose, kind of like when you're fighting with your sibling and one of you swings a little too hard and connects, OUCH! But unlike sibling rivalries, this is a truth that we can benefit from, if we apply it to our lives.

Now prayer is one of *THE* pillars in our walk with God. Prayer is the line of communication that we have with God. Having time that we carve out of our day to spend with God is a major win for us and our relationship with the Lord, or should I say, "wit tha LAWD!".

This block of time is what many people call quiet time, prayer time, or devotional time. I like to call it my "Devo" (if you missed that one, it's just an abbreviation for devotional, catch up yo!).

This time is essential to your spiritual growth because it's a time for you to focus in on your relationship with God and to make "alone time" for God. Let me explain a little more. You see, when you start a relationship or a friendship with someone, the best way for that relationship to grow is for you both to spend time together.

Sometimes the best setting for that is when you are alone, or should I say when you have the least amount of distractions around you. This is what a Devo is, it's time that you intentionally carve out of your day to spend with God, and in doing so, you get to know Him more.

Why is Alone Time So Important?

In one day we experience a lot of changes, with our emotions, and with our behavior. We also hear a lot of voices from people around us and even from ourselves. With life moving at such a rapid pace, we sometimes forget to invest in the relationships that help us stayed centered and focused.

A Devo helps us stay connected with God consistently, while giving us focus as we live every day. It also encourages us and reminds us to keep God first in all that we do. Psalm 27:4-5 says *"I'm asking God for one thing, only one thing: To live with him in his house my whole life long. I'll contemplate his beauty; I'll study at his feet. That's the only quiet, secure place in a noisy world, The perfect getaway, far from the buzz of traffic"* A Devo is a time where we can grow in our faith because we are spending time with the one who not only sustains our faith, but He sustains our life.

What a Devo Looks Like

Let me just throw this out there real quick, just so you know. A Devo doesn't have to look only one way. There are many ways you can structure a Devo, just like there are many ways we can connect with God.

Here are a few ways that you may find helpful as you carve out time to spend with God. Please keep in mind that one of the best things that you can do for yourself and for your relationship with God is to practice having a Devo C-O-N-S-I-S-T-E-N-T-L-Y. My hope is that you carve out time every day to have a Devo, however [comma] if there's a day where it doesn't happen, it's okay, show yourself grace and don't beat yourself up.

All you need to do is say, "Okay, I wasn't intentional in carving out time today, but I will make it a point to carve out time tomorrow". And then actually do it.

Sit down, plan out when you will have your Devo tomorrow, then when tomorrow comes, stick to it. Easy peasy.

Ideas for Devos

Here are a few examples of thing that you can do within your Devo time.

Reflection

This is a time where you choose to reflect. This can include reflecting on the good things that God has done in your life, or even reflecting on things that you feel God has allowed to "stick out" as of late. Reflection is an amazing time to just sort of sit back and think about where you are in God, how you got here, and what God has been doing in your life lately. To reflect is to think back, remember, and truly appreciate who God is and how He's been active in your life. (Psalm 63:6)

Ex. Think about a recent accomplishment, and how God helped you, or how He brought people to you that helped you reach that a goal.

Ask yourself:

1. What did I learn from this?
2. How did I feel while I was in the middle of it all?

3. Where did I see God help me?

Solitude

This is exactly what it sounds like. Putting yourself in a place of solitude or seclusion. Literally going somewhere by yourself, to be by yourself. Often, when we're alone, we are totally exposed to God. This is a time where we are able to be real with God and with ourselves. You can go anywhere, as long as you make it a point to be by yourself or stay to yourself. (Luke 5:16)

Ex. Find time in the day where you can be in your room, by yourself. Turn off your phone and your computer. Get an actual Bible [if you can], journal, or devotional book. You can also go on a walk or to a local area where you can be by yourself or stay to yourself. Try to cut out as many distractions as possible.

In Nature

God created the heavens and the earth, and we have the chance to surround ourselves with it and really take it all in. When we take time to look at what God created, we can learn to really appreciate how big and how smart God is. Along with this, we can think about how this big God who created all of this, loves us. (Psalm 8:3-4)

Ex. Go on a walk at a local park, go hiking at a nearby preserve or mountain. Go kayaking, sometimes slow and steady is really nice, or go to a place where you can see the sunrise or sunset.

Listening to music to worship

Music can move us, it can help us to focus on certain things, and it can also help us express how we feel when we can't find the words. In a Devo, listening to music can be an opportunity to connect with God through lyrics and instruments.

Listening to music that is inspired by or focuses on God can be amazing! My one caution is this, music can help you connect with God, but sometimes it can also distract you from connecting with God. You'll know when it is doing one or the other, and if it distracts you, maybe turn it down, way down, or off. (Psalm 150)

Ex. Go to a place where you can listen to this music. It can be in a room, in a car, or even at an event where there is live music. While the music is playing, you can focus on the lyrics and see how they relate to you.

Journaling

This is you, taking a blank piece of paper, and writing. You can also turn on a recorder or camera and just start talking. Journaling is great because it gives you the chance to express how you feel, even if it doesn't sound perfect or isn't the most polite way to say it, you can just be real. Journaling [let's just call it writing] is a chance for you to be raw, and write the first thing that comes to mind, and then work through those thoughts.

Ex. Get a notebook, go somewhere alone, and write about how your day is going, some of what you saw and experienced and how it made you feel. You can also set up a camera or audio recorder and start talking about those same things. Be real with God and be real with yourself.

Praying

There is so much that we can say about prayer, but I want to keep it simple. Prayer is the communication between you and God. I like to say it this way, prayer is a conversation that you and God can have together. Also, when I say conversation, I mean that. Talk to God like you would your parents or your friends, "Talk regular"!

When I say that, what I mean is don't try to be all fancy and say long words and such. Yes, we are to revere and respect God because of who He is, however He wants us to be honest and real with Him. Sometimes it's hard to do that when we're looking for the perfect words that we think God wants to hear.

Even though prayer is a conversation, sometimes it's good to have certain things that you focus on, such as telling God that you are thankful for this or that. Or, praying that this person would gain peace in their life through God or telling God about a mistake you made, repenting, and receiving His forgiveness.

Ex. One structure that I like to use when I pray is **A.C.T.S.** This stands for

Adoration - telling God how you adore Him, how you love Him,

Confess - Confessing or telling God about your sins, or mistakes you made recently, make a decision to turn away from them [repent], and then receiving his forgiveness

Thanks - Thanking God for what He has given you. Health, family, friends, material things, or recent gains or accomplishments

Supplication- Simply put, that He would SUPPLY, or give you something (promotion, peace in a relationship, or even healing you from an emotional wound)

Reading the Bible

Another great thing that we can spend so much time talking about, but again, I want to keep this simple. Reading the Bible is essential to your growth as a Christian, because it is the Word of God. This means that the entire book was inspired by God. He orchestrated the whole thing, and it's what He created for you to get to know Him.

Reading the bible sometimes sounds like this super heavy thing, but really, no one expects you to memorize the whole thing and know every word cover to cover. So, you can take a deep breath and relax. However, just like any book, the more time you spend reading it, the more you will understand it, and you'll have more questions [questions are okay, you can ask them, seriously].

You can start off with reading small portions, sort of like when you are eating a big meal, you take it one bite at a time. Some scriptures you can write down and start to memorize. These can become "anchors" for you, as in they are scriptures that you are able to remember a little easier than others and you are also able to apply them to your life.

One anchor scripture for me is Jeremiah 17:7, *"Blessed is the man who believes, and trusts in, relies on the Lord; And whose hope and confident expectation is the Lord."* This verse is one I remember often, and it reminds me that when I trust God and when I rely on Him, I will be blessed.

Ex. Start off by reading a little bit at a time each day. That could be a few verses, or that could be a chapter. There are really a lot of places you can start at.
Here are a few:

The Gospels: The books of Matthew, Mark, Luke, then John.

Psalms: Starting at Psalms 1, and reading either a few verses, or a chapter a day

Proverbs: Reading one chapter a day is a really good start. 31 chapters for 30 to 31 days in a month [you catch my drift]

Genesis: Starting at the beginning is smart. I'll be honest, when you get to Leviticus and Deuteronomy, it can seem a little boring, but the more you read it [as you grow in your faith], the more you will appreciate it.

Just Do It!

Like I said earlier, having a Devo is super important, and it's one of the major things that will not only help you grow in your faith, but it will also help sustain you in your relationship with the Lord. I think it's a great idea to carve out time in your day, actually plan it. When that time comes, get away from as many distractions as you can.

I think it's important read the Bible and pray every day. It doesn't have to be an hour or 5 hours, but it is what you make it. You can implement any of these ideas, as long as they bring more quality to your time with God and don't distract you.

Find what works for you and stick to it.

8

Relationships: So Can We Date, or Nah?

So, years ago, when my wife and I met, we were working at a Christian sports camp called Kids Across America [KAA U KNO!], where we used sports as a platform to reach youngsters with the Gospel. I remember the exact moment that we met, we were all getting ready for a 90's theme party for the kids, and our program directors were getting the games together and assigning everyone to stations.

They looked down at their paper and said, "and for the helicopter game we'll have Teshona from the girls side, and........Donte from the boys side." I had no clue who this girl was when I heard her name, but I said "cool." I went over to the station, and I saw her there. I walked up and said, "Hi. I'm Donte." We shook hands, annnnnd that was it. No sparks, no love at first sight, just a handshake.

At that first meeting, I had no clue that we would end up dating and get married two years later. There was one reason I didn't see this coming. It wasn't because I wasn't attracted to her, because I was… like, I WAS! Nor was it because I was dating someone else, because I wasn't. It was because I was in a place in my life where I was content with being single, and I wasn't looking for a relationship, especially a long distance one.

Now this wasn't something that just happened overnight, it took some years for me to see the value of being saved and single, and over that time period I had to come to appreciate my time being single. It was a blessing.

The Transformation

When we get saved, we change, or at least, we should be changing. When we get saved God starts to change our perspective on things. For many of us, we are open to seeing these changes in our lives and we understand why they need to change. However, when it comes to relationships, our perspective doesn't change. This could be because we don't understand why we need to change our perspectives. So, in turn, since we don't have a guide on how to have a relationship as a Christian, we just kind of wing it.

Shortly after I got saved, I began to see my life transform in many areas. However, when it came to dating, I just knew one thing…"Don't be having no sex!" That was it. And that was just something my mama told me, but I really didn't understand why, even after I got saved. It wasn't until years later that I began to understand the transformation that God was doing in my life, how my singleness was a blessing, and how marriage would a blessing.

We should first understand that God saved us and desires to change us because He loves us. He wants us to look more like Him every day. 1st John 2:6 says *"Whoever claims to live in Him, must live as Jesus lived"*

This is the ultimate goal, to look and live more like Jesus. We want that to happen in every area of our life, especially when it comes to relationships. This is why I want to encourage you to remember that no matter what your relationship status is, the goal is to look more like Jesus.

Now that we have that out the way, this is a perfect place to tell you - Don't Rush! I often see folks, single folks and divorcees, get saved, get some insight on who they are and who God is, then want to jump right into a relationship! And for some people in a relationship, they do the same thing and jump right into marriage! Aww snap!

Now I'm not saying that this is bad, or that you have to wait "XX" amount of years before being in a relationship, but what I am saying is make sure you keep the main thing the main thing [looking more like Jesus] and make sure that you are in a healthy place before you start a relationship.

Quick side note, if you want to know if you are in a healthy place, ask God, ask a mentor, and ask as friend. You'll get some truth out of each.

Singleness

Christian and single. There's this thought that if you are single and saved, then you are just lonely, unfulfilled, or that something is wrong with you. I've seen folks have this thinking that if you are a Believer, then you're either dating or looking to date, but no in-between.

The hard part about having this mindset is that when we think like this, it's hard for us to appreciate the time and impact that we have with other people. Instead of embracing this stage of life, we spend our days worrying and hoping for someone to come into our lives so that we can date.

When you are single, I want you to see this time as an opportunity to keep focusing on your relationship with God. You have the ability to devote yourself to God's work without "checking in" with someone. Okay, let me rephrase that. When you are in a relationship, you choose to take on the responsibility of thinking about how someone else fits into your plans.

When you do this, you limit yourself in the freedom you have to do God's work. Now this isn't a bad thing, however, it is a limitation, and when you are single, you are not limited in that area. Paul the apostle, you know that guy that got bit by a poisonous snake a lived (Acts 28:1-6), says that *"Sometimes I wish everyone were single like me—a simpler life in many ways!"* (1 Corinthians 7:7)

Now I know what some people are saying, "I want to fit someone in my schedule! I don't mind checking in, that's what I want!". Don't play yourself! I mean, I feel you, like, I really do feel you! I know what that feeling is like. For many of us, when we're single, we feel that feeling and we just want to have someone we can explore with and be close to. That's not a bad feeling at all. Let me repeat that in case you didn't catch that, IT'S NOT WRONG TO FEEL THAT FEELING!

We have to remember that it will all happen in God's timing. Don't force or try to make it happen on your own. That's when things start to go downhill like a bike with no brakes, and we or someone else, ends up hurt. If you find yourself in a relationship and you have doubts, especially doubts about if this is God's doing or yours, do three things:

1) *Repent* - Let God know that you started something, or the relationship got to a place where He was not the main focus. Confess your fault and receive His forgiveness.

2) *Break-up* - There really is no way around it. If the relationship is unhealthy, or you aren't keeping the main thing the main thing; or you, them, and the relationship ain't growing, then I really don't see any other option. Sometimes we might think, "I can fix this, we can fix this", but again, if God ain't doing the fixing, it's just going to stay broke. And I mean broke BROKE!

3) *Refocus* - simply put, turn your eyes and your focus back on God, and what He wants to do in you and in your life.

If you're here, this is a healthy process that can help you refocus, but the last part may take more time.

Sometimes, being single can be hard, but so can being in a relationship. The thing we have to make sure we're doing is keeping the main thing the main thing [Let's see how many times I can say that in the next 5 pages, *cough cough*]. The main thing is us growing in our faith, and helping others grow in their faith.

When we're single, we're able to devote more time and energy to our relationship with God. We have to choose to recognize singleness as a blessing and not a curse. Singleness can come down to a matter of perspective, and asking the question that the Apostle Paul asks, "Am I content with the Lord? Am I content with where I am?" (Philippians 4:11). If you are single, my hope is that you would see this as an opportunity and a blessing, and that you would embrace where God has you right now, because He is doing great things in you and through you.

Dating

Dating. Courtship. Whatever you call it, let's just jump right into it, ready … GO!

Dating as a Believer can be a really... interesting topic. When we get saved, there is a change in our perspective and in how we think about things. I think that this is an area where either our perspective doesn't change much, or we're not taught a few beneficial lessons in regard to healthy dating. Sometimes, the way we date as Believers is similar to how we date before we got saved, except we implement the "No sex" rule. But why?

I believe that when it comes to dating, we imitate what we see, whether it was what we saw at home, with our friends, or in the media. We just copy and paste [ctrl C then ctrl V. for my nerdy friends, ehh!]. Many times, we don't have a guide on what dating should look like, especially as Believers. This causes us to have baggage from our past relationships. Even "Christian relationships" end with baggage. Let's look at some healthy perspectives when it comes to dating.

Purpose

I met with a young man some time ago and we started talking about the relationship that he was in. He was excited about this young lady! She was beautiful and energetic, and she loved God a lot. As we were talking, he mentioned how he's really enjoying his time with her, and then I asked, "What are your intentions with her?" He looked around and thought for a second, then shrugged his shoulders and said, "I don't really know". I slapped him! [No, just kidding I wouldn't slap anyone. unless they needed it. A nice slap. Like, with just my fingers. Ummm, like a friendly... uhhhhh, let's move on.]

When you start dating someone, it's important to have a purpose in mind, or intentions. Often, I ask the question, "where do you want this relationship to go?" If this question isn't cleared up in the early stages of the relationship, then neither one of you will know where the relationship is going and how you're going to get there.

The reason that this is so important is because when you date someone, you are getting closer to that person's heart, in a very intimate way. Think of it like this, when you date someone, both of your hearts start to transform so that they can go from two separate hearts, into one intimately connected heart [similar to Genesis 2:24].

Even though this is what's supposed to happen in marriage, it starts to happen when you date. Let's say that your heart starts to "join" with someone else's, and you end up breaking up with that person. Your hearts will be ripped from each other, leaving you with a part of your heart missing.

Now, when you date someone else or get married, you go into that new relationship with a part of your heart missing, and not your whole heart, and who only wants part of someone's heart and not the whole thing? NOT ME! The only way to heal our hearts is through repentance and time with God. If we don't take the time to do this, like really, take time, our hearts never fully heal, and we are not able to give all of our heart to one person. Does that make sense?

Remember, you want to be in a place where you can give your all to your future spouse. Now like I said, if you've found yourself in a place where your heart is not whole, you can still be healed and made whole. Repent, and draw close to God, and ask him to heal your heart, and He will, no doubt!

Protect ya' Life

So, when you date, part of your purpose is to protect each other's heart, so that when you and they get married [to each other or to other people], you both can go into that marriage with a whole heart. So here are a few things that you can do, if you are dating or thinking about dating.

1. *Make your intentions known.*

You DON'T have to go into the first date and say, "I'm dating you because I think you could be my spouse." First off, slap yourself, 'cause that's a bad look homie. Secondly, when you allow your intentions to be known, especially early on, you both can be on the same page, and there aren't as many surprises. Plus, you waste less time with someone who is not on the same page as you. Make it plain yo.

2. *Set up boundaries*

This is a MAJOR KEY!!! You see, when you get into a relationship, most people just kind of let it go wherever it goes, emotionally, physically, and even spiritually. This is a little dangerous because if there are no guidelines laid out, then you seriously have no clue where this relationship could end up, and that's not what you want! [Trust me on this one!]

It's important to set some boundaries, for you and for your partner. Again, the reason you set boundaries is so that you can protect each other's hearts. With this, you can

have a relationship that honors God. Here's a very short list
of examples for boundaries.

    a. Only go on dates and hang out in public places, where
it's more than just you two.

    b. Limit the amount of time that you spend together. You
may really enjoy each other, but remember, you got friends,
and other responsibilities. Just don't be caked up ALL the
time. *enters "caked up" into Urbandictionary.com*

    c. Slow down the conversation. Try not to talk too much
about what ya'lls future together looks like. For example,
"Let's have ## kids" and "When we get married let's
vacation at …" It's a little too much, you feel me. I'm not
saying don't talk about these things, but just make sure the
timing is right, don't rush. Enjoy each other today.

    d. Limit Physical touching. Holding hands, kissing, all of
that. It may be best to put a boundary on that. This is
important because not doing so could lead you to being
physically intimate in a way that does not honor God. And
that could just flat out wreck you in the end!

3. Pray.

Make sure that you are praying about and for your relationship. Don't think "Well, I'm saved, they're saved, so we're good!" NOPE! That's not always the case. Take time to pray about your relationship and ask people that you trust to pray for you also.

4. Get mentors.

Yeah……….. Go do that right now! First, it would be a great idea to have individual mentors, two people that are not a couple. These mentors can give you wisdom from their perspective, and they'll only have to focus on you.

Then after that, when you are in the right place in your relationship, you can get a "couple mentor", two Believers that are married [preferably more than 5 years]. They can give you perspective about long term relationships, mutual goals, and things you should think about before you talk about marriage.

5. Don't' be having No SEX!

Soooo, Yeah. I just said it. Don't be having no sex! *BUT WHY NOT?!* You see, God created sex to be enjoyed within marriage. And since you are not married, it's best that you don't have sex. It really just makes the relationship more difficult.

Sex is like sports [sort of]. When you play a sport with the rules in place, you get the best enjoyment out of it. But when someone cheats or breaks the rules, it starts to lose its interest and become less fun. God has guidelines about sex, and when we follow them, it's enjoyable [just trust me on this one]. But when the rules are broken, it's just not the same.

[Side note: If you have already had sex in your relationship, or in another relationship, there is grace for you. Please don't be all "Woe is me", "I'm damaged goods", No! Stop! When you sincerely repent, seek spiritual and emotional healing, then choose to follow God's guidelines and instructions, you are redeemed, you are made whole, and most of all, you are forgiven.]

Lastly, whether you are in a relationship or not, choose to be where you are and keep your eyes on the Lord. For some people, God has called you to be single, and for others He has called you to be in a relationship. Both can truly be a blessing and help you grow in your relationship with the Lord.

Either way, just don't force it.

9

The Gray(ish) Area

When we get saved, we start to see the world differently. Well, it takes a bit of time for this to happen. The funny thing is there is something inside of us that just starts to kind of know some of the things that we should and shouldn't do. I want to say that this is the Holy Spirit that's leading us and showing us what's really good, or beneficial for us.

The problem we run into is that we sometimes start to do things [or not do things] on our own, and the Holy Spirit is not leading us at all. Remember the Holy Spirit, the one who leads us to truth and a good understanding of things? (John 16:13-15)

Now don't get me wrong, YES, the Holy Spirit will help us understand things that are right and wrong, but He will also help us understand what is beneficial for us. BUT! There are sometimes in our lives where we do things or stop doing things because we think they are right or wrong, and we really don't have a good understanding of why.

The great thing about having the Holy Spirit in our lives is that we will begin to understand things a bit clearer, it may take some time to get there, but we will. One of the major things that the Holy Spirit helps us understand is this, "What can I do as a Believer and what can't I do?", or "What are things that I can keep in my life, and what are some things that I need to get rid of?".

What are some things that we need to give up and what's some stuff that we can keep? When I say give up and keep, I'm talking about everything from "Can I keep this T.V. show in my life?", to "Can I keep this attitude toward this person?".

Like I said earlier, the Bible tells us that if we want to live like Jesus, we have to start walking and living like He did (1 John 2:6). This also means that there are some things in our lives that we do that are not helping us live more like Jesus.

I'm not saying that we have to be perfect, but I'm saying that we should be walking toward perfection. You don't have to be "sinless", but you should be trying to "sin less". Walking this line can be a little tricky, so let's walk through understanding this together and get a little more clarity.

Legalism? What's That?

Let's start here! Legalism! *"What does that mean?"* I'm glad you asked. Legalism is…. Hmm, what's a simple way of putting it. Legalism is doing everything that YOU think is right as a Christian, and not doing what YOU think is wrong as a Christian, AND trying to force other people to think the same way YOU think about these legal and illegal things.

For example, Legalism is thinking that going to the movies is bad, and then judging other people that go to the movies simply because YOU think it's bad. What makes legalism worse is that you not only do what YOU think is right and wrong, but you also think that God thinks the same way, and that God will only love you if you do this "right" stuff and not the "wrong" stuff. It's a TRAP!

The thing about legalism that gets people caught up is that they do and don't do things because they think that these things are what makes God happy and makes Him love us. It becomes a "check the box" game. "Did I pray today? Check. Did I do 2 acts of kindness today? Check. Did I not go to the movies? Check. Okay, God loves me today!" You see the problem here?

You do things because you feel like you have to in order for God to love you. Your life becomes these boxes that you check every day, and if you don't check them all, you think that God doesn't love you that day. This is a major problem because this is SO far from the truth.

God love us, God loves you, point, blank, period. In the Bible, Romans 5:8 tells us that *"But God demonstrates His own love for us in this: While we were still sinners, Christ died for us"* This means that God loved you, even before you were saved, and just because you are saved now doesn't mean that you have to "work" for His love, He already loves you. So, legalism is bad, because it makes you do things, and it forces you to do what YOU think is right. The truth is, God ain't forcing nobody to do nothing.

Over-Gracified

Now with all of that said, that doesn't mean that we can just do whatever we want. When I was 16, one of my close friends, who claimed to be saved, said "Yeah, having sex might be wrong as a Christian, but hey, God's gonna forgive me anyways, right?" well... that's not quite right. God loves us no doubt, but that doesn't mean that God loves everything that we do. I love my 4-year-old daughter so much! But I'm not a fan of when she writes on the T.V. and then saying "Wow Daddy, I don't know how that got there!" When she does that, I don't love her any less, I'm just not a fan of that decision.

I believe that God is very similar in that He loves us, but there are some things that we do that He's not a fan of, sin. Yet, when we sin, He doesn't love us any less, but He still wants us to "sin less". He knows that it's a process, He knows it takes time, and He is patient. God forgives our sin when we repent, but just because He does, doesn't mean that we can just sin and do whatever we want. Romans 6:1 says *"So what do we do? Keep on sinning so God can keep on forgiving? I should hope not!"*

Legalism is bad because it's all about checking the box, but the flip side of that is called "Antinomianism" (anti-No-me-ah-Nizm), but because I don't like using big words, let's just say "grace grace grace". "Grace Grace Grace" is bad because it takes the grace and patience that God freely shows us, and warps it into this idea that "Oh, I can do whatever I want because... there's grace, right?" WRONG!

We don't want to abuse God's grace because it just shows that we don't respect God or that we don't care what He thinks [I mean really, when you think about it]. If my daughter pours Orange juice on the floor on purpose [Yes, she has], I will show her grace and patience. But if I tell her "Hey love, please don't do that", and she keeps doing it anyways, that shows me that she either doesn't respect what I am saying, or she doesn't care. And that's not a good look.

So now that we have a better understanding of legalism and "Grace Grace Grace", let's look for that happy medium.

Happy Medium(ish)

The happy medium is a [Holy]Spirit led search for truth that pleases God. It's us doing things that God calls us to do, but doing them from our heart, and not because we are forced to. It's asking the Holy Spirit to help us understand why we should or shouldn't do something, and also going to the Bible for answers too.

[Side note, it's okay to question or ask questions about your faith and your conduct. You don't have to follow along blindly and just do what the pastor or preacher tells you to do!! You can go find the answers.

That's totally fine, because the more you understand, the more you see the bigger picture, and the more grounded you'll be about your faith.

On the flip side, don't ignore what pastors say to you just because you don't want to hear it. This can lead you to making up what you want to hear, and that's no good. Now, let's resume to our regularly written program.]

The medium is, I do it because I believe that I can do it, and I choose to. I don't do some things because they're not beneficial to me. For example, I read my Bible because I want to, because I know that it will bring me closer to God and help me understand my faith better. Even when I don't feel like it, I do it because I know that it adds value to my life and my faith.

I don't watch horror movies because for me, it's not beneficial. Even though horror movies are everywhere, I still find no benefit from them. It doesn't help me understand my faith, nor is it a preference of mine. There may be some things that apply to you, maybe it's watching certain types of movies or drinking alcoholic drinks.

At some point you'll have to process through them to see where you are with them and if they fall into the happy medium place, where you are Spirit led to your answer. Now, how do you process through these things to get to a place where you can get an answer.

Different people have different processes. Let me share with you my process for this. This is my general process of how I come to understand things that I should and shouldn't do. I hope that it gives you some direction.

First, ask the question. Should I or shouldn't I...
Watch this movie
Drink this drink
Go to this small group
Go to this place
Have this conversation
Listen to this music
Pray or Read my Bible
Get this tattoo...etc

Most of these types of questions have to do with what we are doing or how we should conduct ourselves. Now, here are the questions that I ask when I start to process and get to my answer.

What does the Bible say?

Ask if the Bible clearly states an answer on this.

You can read the bible, look up scriptures on the topic, or even Google "what does the bible say about…" Try to find multiple sources, such as sermons, scriptures, blogs, even ask your friends and mentors [the ones that have sense, you feel me].

Is it legal?

Flat out, is what I'm thinking legal. I think that's an easy one to find out.

Will it hurt someone?

If there is something you want to do, or you are asking how you should approach something, think about if it will hurt someone. This is more along the lines of how to conduct yourself as far as your attitude, or conversation, etc.

What's the purpose of it?

Why do you want to this thing? Will this add value to you or your faith? Sometimes when we actually ask ourselves why, we really find the motive of why we want to do something.

Am I mature enough for this?

Ask the question, "Am I mature enough to do this thing?" You can also ask yourself, "Am I even mature enough to process through this without jumping to one side or the other?" These are the questions where sometimes you just know if you are or not, but you have to be real with yourself about it, especially if you are not ready for it.

Here's an example.

When I was 20 years old, I wanted to get a tattoo, and I used this process. After really taking a hard look at what the Bible says, then asking "is it legal", and the next few questions, I thought that it was okay. But then I realized that at the time, I wasn't mature enough to make that decision, truthfully, I was too emotional. So, I processed through it off and on for about 2 years, and then I got to a place where I felt that I was mature and, in a place, where I had understanding. It was the happy medium place.

This was something that "I" had to process through. Please, don't just take my word or someone else's word on these things, and don't rationalize and say "oh I can do this" when you really aren't sure. Take time and process. This process is different for me, and it'll be different for you. Try not to overthink everything, but in some of these tough, grayish areas, process through it.

<u>Final Notes</u>

As things change, and as you get closer to God and grow in your faith, your thinking will change on some things. As you process through these thoughts, be real with yourself and be honest with God. It'll take time to really think through some of these things, but as you do it more often, the process will become a little smoother.

Romans 14:22-24 says, *"You may believe there's nothing wrong with what you are doing, but keep it between yourself and God. Blessed are those who don't feel guilty for doing something they have decided is right. But if you have doubts about whether or not you should eat something, you are sinning if you go ahead and do it. For you are not following your convictions. If you do anything you believe is not right, you are sinning"*

For clarity, Paul wrote this, and was talking to Believers back in the day about whether it was right to eat meat [it was a cultural thing]. But I think this principle applies to us. Process through what you think and believe, keep it between you and God, and if you doubt, even just a little bit, you're better off just chillin' and not doing it. But if there is no guilt, great!

Keep it between you and God and be blessed.

10

God's Sovereignty

Understanding this core principle of God's sovereignty gives us the ability to walk this walk in such a free way. Hold'on now, this is a big word, but it's so important, we must come to know about God's sovereignty [You gotta sound it out homie, Saah-Vren-TeE!]. Sovereignty means supreme power, and in this case, it means that God has all power.

The way I remember this is Sovereign (Saah-vREN) = "So Rain". Now let me snap this down to size for you, and also briefly tackle one of the biggest questions that many people have about God, which is "If God is good, why do bad things happen?" I promise this will all connect, stick with me.

If God is Good, Why Do Bad Things Happen?

So many people ask this question, "if God is good, why do bad things happen?" This question is asked by scholars and incredible thinkers, all the way to Bob, the guy standing in front of you at the grocery store. I think the reason that so many of us have this same question is two-fold.

1) We've been told or taught that God is good, plain and simple. No matter how things look in the world or in our lives, someone has been there saying "God is good child!"

2) While we've been told that God is good, we still see bad things happening all over the world, in our own communities, even in our own lives. You will always get a question like this when you are told one thing, but you see evidence that can make it look false.

Why do bad things happen if God is good and if He is so powerful? Well, let's start with this, God is good. There are good things in this world. Like love, like breathing, like ICE CREAM!! These are seen as good things by many people, and they all start with God either creating them, or allowing them to be created by someone, like ice cream. Got it? Good! Now, why do bad things happen? They happen because God gives humans choices. "*HUH?!?!?*" Hear me out.

God is good, and inside of that goodness is Him giving us the option to make choices, and not forcing us to do things. We call this free will. If God forced us to do things, He wouldn't really be seen as good, right? He gives us a choice. Just like when we think of Adam and Eve eating the "forbidden fruit" (Genesis 3). God could have forced them not eat it, or He could've destroyed that tree all together, but He gave them a choice.

God gives us a choice because His desire is to love us and for us to choose to love Him. Can we truly love God if we are forced to, or if there really aren't any other options? Is that real love? I don't think so.

So back to it, bad things happen because God's goodness gives us the option to choose what we want to do, to love or to hate, to heal or to hurt, to listen to and follow Him, or to do things on our own. We have the choice. And yes, God still does have all power.

"But how can God have all power but still give us a choice?".

Its simple [sort of], because While He *allows* us to choose, and He *allows* things to happen. It's not either or, it's both and. It's not "God has all power, or he gave us all free will", but it's "God has all power AND He gives us free will."

God *allowed* Adam and Eve to choose between trusting Him and not trusting Him, which led to sin coming into the world. It's the sin in the world, it's the sin that is in our hearts as human beings, that causes us to choose to do things that could hurt other people.

Now, can God stop us from doing these things and stop all these bad things from happening? Well, He could, but would He still be good? Can He love us and not give us a choice to do good or bad? Could we still choose to love Him even if we had no other choice at all?

God's desire is to love us, and He wants us to love him back. The only way that love can be true, genuine, and real is if we are given the choice to love. Let's be clear, God doesn't cause these bad things, He doesn't look at somebody and say "I'm going to make sure they have a terrible day today! Just because I'm God!" No, it doesn't work like that. God *allows* things to happen, good and bad.

One other important thing to note is that when something bad or unfortunate happens, it ain't always God. He's not sitting back waiting for you to "mess up" so He can punish you, that's not God. Not even close. So now, "So rain." [Let me explain]

When it rains, we all get wet. It doesn't matter who you are, how much money you have, or what ethnicity you are, none of that matters when it rains. In the same way, when the sun shines, it shines on everyone, no matter who you are, no matter how much money you have, or what ethnicity you are. You still feel the sun shine on you!

So, what is God's sovereignty? It's Him having all power and allowing things to happen. Yes, God is powerful enough to cause things to happen and to stop things from happening. However, God also allows things to happen. Meaning, if He wants to stop something He can, however often times He gives us a choice.

Now we have to remember that people are naturally sinful, and it's the sin in us that causes us to think of only ourselves and to do things that hurt others. God gives us the choice to do good or to do bad. He gives us the choice, and it's up to us to choose what we want to do with that choice.

All Things Work Together

Now that we have a better understanding of God's sovereignty, I want you know that as things are happening in your life, as you experience joy and pain, God is working out everything that's happening for your good. No matter what you are going through, good or bad, joyful or difficult, God is working in the background for you, and He is on your side.

In Romans 8:28, Paul says that *"And we know that in all things God works for the good of those who love him, who have been called according to his purpose"*

All. Things. Work. Together.

So, as you are growing in your faith, and walking with God, remember that regardless of where you are in your walk, God is with you, cheering you on, and wanting you to be successful in life and in your walk with Him.

As you walk this walk, focus on God, and focus on God's goodness. Yes, sin does play a factor in our lives, and in the lives of all of man-kind, but as Believers, we aren't ruled by sin anymore! We are free through the power of God! When you focus on God, you start to focus less on sin, and that's the point!

So, remember, spend more time looking at God than you do looking at the problem. Don't spend time thinking and focusing only on sin, trying to avoid sin, and trying not to mess up, because God's not waiting in the bushes to jump out and laugh at you when you do sin. He's there, with you, loving you, and rooting for you.

You got this!

11

Choosing Life

"When you get saved, everything _____ !"

Did you get it? One of the big themes we've been choppin' it up about the past few chapters, <u>Everything CHANGES</u>! It's crazy to think about all of the things that have changed in your life [and mine] since we got saved and started our personal relationship with Jesus.

Now that we are walking the walk, we are now seeing some of those big and small changes happen in our lives. I mean, just take a sec and think about some of the things that have happened over the past few weeks for you.

Do you notice a change in your Christian walk, or maybe in your confidence? What about the people that you are around now, are they different than what they were before you got saved? I think that this is one of the most powerful things about becoming a Christian, the fact that your life seriously changes, and you do things differently now than you did before you got saved. That's crazy! Like, Rubik's cube solved in 5 seconds kind of crazy!

One other crazy thing to think about is that now that you are saved, your thoughts are even different. Things that you believed, or thought were okay, you now look at and say "What was I thinkin' man!?" That's a good thing, because this shows that your mind, and your thoughts, are changing; or another term to use is that they are "being renewed".

Just to be clear, you still have the same brain, the same "you" shaped head, and all the memories that you have are still in there. Now, as you move forward in your walk with Jesus, you see the world a little differently. You might also start thinking a little differently. One thing that I want to encourage you to do as you grow, is to choose life.

Choose Life

"What the HECK does that mean, Choose Life?" Let me tell you, or as Fire Marshall Bill used to say, "Let me show'ya something!" In our lives, we are always faced with choices. Some are more important than others. Some choices are like "What do I want for breakfast" or "should I wear my blue hat or my gray hat today?" Easy right [the blue one of course!]. Even though many of these choices don't have any major consequences, it does remind us that every day, we will have a lot of choices to make. Just as some are as simple as which hat to wear, some are a bit more serious like "should I spend time this this person today?" or "should I pray today?"

These choices you make will have a bigger impact on how you feel emotionally today and how you'll grow as a Believer. And It's important to remember that with each choice you make, you are creating a habit. The old adage is "Your choice leads to an act, your act leads to a habit, your habits lead to a character, and your character leads to a destiny."

To choose life means to choose the things that will bring you closer to God and push you away from sin. Choosing life means to choose things that will help you create positive habits, noble character, and a God-led destiny. When you choose life in the little things, it will help you to choose life in the big things. When you make it a habit to choose life over and over and over again, you'll start producing results in your life that are positive and God-led, and you'll start seeing how choosing life is good for you.

What You Choosin'?

In the Old Testament, in Deuteronomy 30, Moses
was talking to His people and tells them that God said
*"Today I ask heaven and earth to be witnesses. I am
offering you life or death, blessings or curses. Now, choose
life! Then you and your children may live. To choose life is
to love the Lord your God, obey him, and stay close to him.
He is your life, and He will let you live many years in the
land, the land he promised to give your ancestors
Abraham, Isaac, and Jacob"*

So, in a nutshell, Moses is saying that today, if you
choose life, meaning love God, obey and follow Him, you
will be blessed! But if you choose not to, then you are
choosing death, you are choosing the opposite of blessings,
which are curses. I know this might sounds extreme, but I
think this is spot on. This is one of the most important
things that we have to do as Believers. We have to choose
life!

The reason this is important is because our mission
as Believers is to grow closer to God, and to love other
people just like God loves us. The only way we can do that
is if we start to think like He does and do the things that He
does. Every day we have the chance to make the choice to

read our Bible or to not read our Bible, to forgive people or to not forgive people.

Every day we have these choices, and I want to encourage you to make the choice to choose life today. To bless others with your time and energy, to grow closer to God through spending time with Him. Along with this, do things that will spread the love of God to the people around you.

Don't Over Think it Fam

Now that we have a better understanding of what it means to choose life, I think it's only fitting to tell you Don't Over Think IT! It's important to remember that it all starts with your mind, AND! It's a process.

When you choose life, when you choose do those beneficial things, you are "choosing", meaning you are making up your mind about something. Now, that may sound like a simple task, but remember, you are faced with hundreds of choices a day, and some may be super easy while others are... let's just say not easy. When you get to those decisions that are "not easy", you sometimes have to pause and think for a quick sec, am I choosing life? Or nah? Sometimes it just comes down to that.

There are times where we, as Believers, get so caught up in the actions and the results of things, that we forget that it starts with us making our minds up about somethings. Example, Should I forgive my brother for what he said to me last week? Hmm, let me think, choosing life = choosing God. God forgave me and tells me to forgive others. Choose life.

Now, when it comes to the actions, we may not always be comfortable with the particular action that is needed. We may not always enjoy choosing the right thing, but it helps shape the rest of our thinking and our actions. When I choose life, and say, "I'm making up my mind and reading my Bible today", then I start to think about the when, the where, and if I need to rearrange my schedule. With this, I start to line my actions up with what I choose. Again, this is why it's important to remember that our choices start in our mind, then the actions and other thoughts will follow.

What makes this interesting, especially when we are being truthful, is that this is a process that takes time to learn, to do, and to make it a habit of. The reason I say that we have to be truthful is because it is very easy to say "I want to choose life, but I know it's a process that takes time, so I don't have to choose life right now, I can do it later." Hmmm, if you're thinking that, take your hand, raise it up, and slap yourself! [I've had to do that plenty of times]

I think I should start this by saying that yes, it is a process, but this doesn't give us room to slack off when we feel like it. Remember, grace is there for when we need it, not when we want it. We don't want to get caught up in Grace Grace Grace!

So yeah, choosing life is a process that you'll learn to do while you grow as a Believer. You won't be perfect at it, and that's okay. Jesus was the only person to choose life, all the time, and frankly, you're not Jesus. So, give yourself grace as you learn how to choose life every day.

Do Your Best, Forget the Rest

Every day is a new day, the Bible says "Certainly the faithful love of the Lord hasn't ended; certainly, God's compassion isn't through! They are renewed every morning. Great is your faithfulness." (Lamentations 3:22-23). That means that every day, God is rooting for you, and He's there to help you choose life. Even when you fall short or mess up, God is still there.

It reminds me of my daughter again, I want her to choose to do the right things, but I know that she may not always do that. Still, I never point a finger at her or make her feel bad because she didn't choose the right thing. I just show her grace and love, and let her know "Hey kid, it's okay. This doesn't change how I feel about you. Now let's just move forward and we can try again."

Yes, God's desire is for us to choose life every day, but He also knows that we are going to trip up every now and again, that's why He is so gracious to us. His desire is also for us to do our best. I like to say, "do you best and forget the rest!"

Do your best and forget about your past mistakes. Do your best and forget about when you last got tripped up. Now, remember that you can still learn something from those mistakes, but don't let them hang over you and bring you down. Forget about it, better yet, Fa'get about'eht!

Do your best, Grow closer to God, and Choose life.

Final Thoughts

Well family, here we are at the end of our journey together for now. It has truly been a pleasure and an honor to be able to walk alongside of you as you grow in your faith. I am blessed and humbled that you would pick up this book and take a little wisdom from it, and some practical things that will help you grow strong.

I want to encourage you to always stay close to the Lord, no matter what! He is there for you, and He is your loving Father that wants to see you succeed in all that you do.

I pray that you've not only learned a lot, but that you have actually put some of what you've learned into practice. This book, and many other books [sermons, blogs, podcasts] are only as good as you allow them to be in your life.

You can listen to and read as much content as your heart desires, but at the end of the day fam, if you aren't applying what you are learning, or letting it sink into your heart, then you might be better off staring at a wall. For real though!

So please, put into practice what you are learning, and what God is teaching you. I'm not here to give you the complete list of "This is what you need to do to be a Christian", but these are just some of the things that I've been able to learn, and things that have helped me in my walk with the Lord.

There is still a whole lot to learn, but remember, it's a marathon, it's not a sprint. Stay the course homie, and don't give up.

I love you, God loves you, and You got this.

About the Author

Donte Allen has been a believer for nearly 15 years. After making a genuine commitment to God, Donte has been at the front lines of the faith, working in youth ministry for over 10 years, and as a Licensed Pastor for 5 years.

His humble beginnings and desire for learning have shaped him to be hungry and humble yo. He was born ad raised in St. Louis, MO, establish his family in Whitewater, WI, and now resides in Sunny California.

Donte is married to the love of his life, Teshona, and they have one sassy'n sweet daughter, Nissi. He is truly thankful to his family, and the community that invested in his life in Whitewater, WI.

Made in the USA
Columbia, SC
03 August 2018